FOR YOUR HOME

BLUE & WHITE ROOMS

FOR YOUR HOME

BLUE & WHITE ROOMS

Ann Rooney Heuer

FRIEDMAN/FAIRFAX

PUBLISHERS

Dedication

For my loving family circle: Fred, "Beana," Elizabeth, Francis, and Ellen...and for the heavenly creator, who has painted an infinite universe of color and beauty.

Acknowledgments

My sincere thanks to my editors, Reka Simonsen and Valerie Kennedy, and to the many designers, architects, artists, and photographers whose creative visions have helped inspire this international celebration of two of the world's richest and most revered colors.

A FRIEDMAN/FAIRFAX BOOK

©1998 by Michael Friedman Publishing Group, Inc.

Library of Congress Cataloging-in-Publication data available upon request.

ISBN 1-56799-732-5

Editor: Reka Simonsen
Art Director: Jeff Batzli
Layout Designer: Meredith Miller
Photography Editor: Valerie E. Kennedy
Production Manager: Camille Lee

Color separations by Fine Arts Repro House Co., Ltd.
Printed in Hong Kong by Midas Printing Limited

1 3 5 7 9 10 8 6 4 2

For bulk purchases and special sales, please contact:
Friedman/Fairfax Publishers
Attention: Sales Department
15 West 26th Street
New York, New York 10010
212/685-6610 FAX 212/685-1307

Visit our website:
http://www.metrobooks.com

Table of Contents

INTRODUCTION

When I was five, I thought the prettiest shades of blue were in the tiny forget-me-nots and climbing morning glories of my parents' garden. Nearly twenty summers later, while honeymooning in Bermuda, I was romanced by the more dazzling blue of the aquamarine Atlantic Ocean. And then, one beautiful autumn in Illinois, my husband and I discovered the most precious blue of all—the luminous ultramarine of our newborn daughter's eyes.

Chances are good that a variety of blues will remind you of beautiful things, breathtaking landscapes, and the people you love. Around the world, blue magically captivates, for it is a regal hue with a rich history. Just as revered, however, is the combination of blue and white, a contrasting duet of colors that is always exciting and refreshing. For centuries, alluring shades of indigo, cobalt, turquoise, and robin's-egg blue have dovetailed with white in priceless Chinese porcelains, exotic Moroccan tiles, lovely Dutch delft china, French toile de Jouy fabric, cozy American quilts, and lyrical paintings by celebrated artists.

The color blue has been highly regarded through the ages, not only for its beauty, but because for many centuries it was a rare luxury. To create an ultramarine paint for royal palaces, temples, and tombs, the ancient Egyptians would grind precious lapis lazuli stones into fine powder, or dissolve compounded copper salts with resin. Later, the ancient Greeks produced a wider range of blues by experimenting with copper, iron, and mercury. It wasn't until the twelfth century A.D. that ultramarine was introduced to Europe, and even then, it was so expensive that it was only used by painters. By the eighteenth century, however, the British East India Company imported affordable indigo dyes to Europe, and Prussian blue, the first synthetic blue pigment, was produced. During the Victorian era, new synthetic dyes added blue-greens and purples to the rainbow of textile and paint colors.

Historically, many civilizations have considered blue and white to be enriching or virtuous colors. To early Egyptians, blue represented celestial light and justice. In

Opposite: DETAILS SUCH AS THE FEDERAL SHIELD-BACK ARMCHAIR, THE STRIPED BLUE AND WHITE WALLPAPER, AND THE LOVELY BALLOON SHADES ADD A SENSE OF YESTERDAY TO THIS ELEGANTLY APPOINTED LIVING ROOM.

ancient Greece, blue stood for altruism and integrity, while white denoted purity. During the Middle Ages, the Church believed that white symbolized purity and blue represented spiritual love or truth.

Today, blue is a color that signifies tranquillity, spirituality, trustworthiness, and infinity. Bold, vivid blues are also associated with high drama and energy. White is a valuable neutral color that comes in numerous shades, from bright titanium to gentle magnolia, vanilla, ivory, and cream. White can contrast smartly with royal or navy blues. It can also soften blue's bold personality and create a visual resting point in a room.

Whatever blissful blue and white interiors you envision, it's helpful to remember that blue's refreshing coolness is greatly affected by surrounding hues. It's important to pay attention to color temperature when decorating: blue, green, and violet are the cool colors of the spectrum, while red, orange, and yellow are warm hues that radiate more light and heat. By following a few simple guidelines you can warm your blue and white palette and avoid unintentionally creating a melancholy room.

Be sure to consider your room's lighting. If its windows face north, the room will likely receive limited, bluish-toned light that needs to be perked up with accents in warm colors such as yellow or scarlet. On the other hand, a southern exposure will probably be sunny and appropriate for dazzling, pure blue and white schemes. Also, keep in mind that incandescent light bulbs can add a warm, yellow glow, while fluorescent fixtures will cool the atmosphere with pale blue light, and halogen lamps may sap the richness from your colors.

Before you pick up a paintbrush or look for a new wallpaper pattern, it's a good idea to immerse yourself in a sea of blue and white possibilities. The following pages will take you across the globe and back through time to explore eight decorating styles that offer captivating interpretations of the blue and white theme: traditional Federal, Regency, and Victorian styles; distinctive country styles from North America, Scandinavia, France, and the Mediterranean; and the clean contemporary style.

America's Federal style, which was popular in the late eighteenth and early nineteenth centuries, was a celebration of America's status as a powerful, expanding young republic. The Federal style was inspired by the neoclassical decors and furnishings of the French Empire and English Regency styles, but often incorporated such patriotic symbols as the eagle instead of traditional classic motifs.

The elegant, airy English Regency style came into vogue when George IV became Prince Regent in 1811. Regency style took inspiration from the architecture and colors of ancient Greece and Rome, as well as the regal French Empire style popularized during Napoleon's reign. Vibrant contrasting colors were paired together, which complemented furnishings and architectural moldings that incorporated such ancient motifs as honeysuckles, lyres, shells, and Greek keys.

Above, left: WHILE WHITE AND PASTEL BLUES VISUALLY ENLARGE A LIVING SPACE, DARKER BLUES ADVANCE, MAKING A ROOM APPEAR MORE INTIMATE. THIS CONTEMPORARY KITCHEN ACHIEVES A SENSE OF COZINESS WITH ITS DEEP THISTLE-BLUE CABINETS, WHICH CONTRAST BEAUTIFULLY WITH WHITE CUPBOARDS AND TILES AND A PALE WOODEN COUNTER. **Above, right:** ROYAL BLUE PAINT HAS BEEN SPONGED ON THE WALLS OF THIS COMBINED LIBRARY AND DINING ROOM, GIVING A CONTEMPORARY TWIST TO THE TRADITIONAL NEOCLASSICAL DECOR. THE BRIGHT WHITE FIREPLACE IS EMBELLISHED WITH IONIC "COLUMNS."

Interiors of the Victorian period were often done in dark, rich, earthy colors—a sharp contrast to the bright hues of the Regency era. Formal rooms were dressed in a plethora of patterns, colors, and ornaments. Flora and fauna wallpapers were favored, as were plush fabrics with tassels, overstuffed upholstery, knickknacks, and heavy, dark wooden furnishings.

Blue and white have been the colors of choice for numerous country decorating schemes, warming up eclectic gatherings of faded furnishings and the rustic textures of wood, brick, and stone. American country style is known for its array of simple wooden furnishings and muted milk-paint hues. Blue and white are popular colors for such key accessories as patchwork quilts, braided rugs, and graniteware.

Scandinavian country style is easily recognized by its furniture painted with floral designs (called rosemaling), its use of bright colors as accents, and its preference for light-colored woods. Scandinavian style was popularized around 1900 by Swedish artist Carl Larsson. He detested dark, cluttered Victorian decors and wanted to introduce a pleasant, orderly mix of simple furnishings and pale hues that would reflect maximum light—sunshine is a precious commodity in Scandinavian countries.

Both French and Mediterranean country styles are awash in vivid hues appropriate to a sun-drenched climate. French country originated in Provence, which is known for its fragrant flowers and herbs as well as its lively cotton prints and charming style of decor. The wide Mediterranean Sea has inspired another style of vibrant country decor. The clean, spare looks of this style, with its thick, white walls of stone or plaster and weathered blue doors and shutters, can be seen throughout southern Europe and northern Africa.

In a contemporary setting, blue and white create a crisp ambience that is invigorating and fresh. Clean lines and minimal furnishings and accessories often characterize contemporary decors, which celebrate light, texture, color, and form, taking inspiration from any number of simple, elegant decorating styles. A myriad of vivid blue and white appliances, furnishings, wall and floor treatments, and fabrics featuring geometric prints and sprawling patterns have indeed created a look that's both atmospheric and inviting.

Opposite: THIS AMERICAN COUNTRY BEDROOM EVOKES SEASIDE COTTAGE MEMORIES WITH ITS IRIS BLUE, INDIGO, AND WHITE FABRICS AND ACCESSORIES. THE WHALE MOTIF IN THE FRAMED PRINTS IS REPEATED IN THE CURTAINS.

Tranquil Outdoor Living Spaces and Enchanted Gardens

White, ivory, gray-blue, and teal are colors that blend effortlessly with earth and sky, so it's not surprising that more and more homeowners are choosing these soft, natural hues. Porches and other outdoor living spaces are in vogue again, as are tranquil garden "rooms" in summery blues and whites.

White has long been a favorite color choice for the façades of contemporary and country homes, as well as traditional Colonial, Greek Revival, and Victorian houses. These typically feature contrasting blue, black, or green shutters and matching front doors. The façades of more ornate Victorian homes, however, may feature up to five different hues, sometimes incorporating a palette of pale and medium blues and whites.

White is also a popular choice for any number of country- and contemporary-style homes around the world. Countless French and Mediterranean country homes reflect the dazzling sun with thick, whitewashed or tinted stucco walls accented with brightly painted azure shutters and doors and warm terra-cotta tiled roofs and courtyards. In Scandinavia, country home interiors may feature resplendent pale blue walls, but the timber exteriors are often painted red, yellow, or green, accentuated by white shutters and gingerbread trim.

No matter what shade your home's façade wears, it can serve as a lovely backdrop for such outdoor living spaces as porches, patios, decks, courtyards, terraces, gazebos, and loggias, which are columned, open-air spaces on the side of a home. Also, if you live in a temperate climate, you can create a lush "outdoor" room inside your home with a glass-enclosed conservatory or sunroom. The conservatory was especially beloved

Opposite: This Mediterranean-inspired outdoor space is a symphony in blue with custom-designed blue and white tile murals and a dazzling pool.

during the Victorian era and is enjoying renewed popularity today in Europe and North America. The sunroom has also become a popular "greenhouse" space where flowers and families can soak up winter sunshine together. Blue and white are the ideal hues for any of these sanctuaries and can be introduced through a variety of paints, tiles, floorings, furnishings, and accessories.

Wooden porches, loggias, and gazebos can be painted or stained white, cream, blue, or silvery gray, while their ceilings can be painted a pale blue and airbrushed with wisps of white clouds to suggest the ethereal heavens. This decorating tradition was popular during the Victorian era and was inspired by the lifelike painted ceilings favored during the Renaissance.

If your home is graced with an open-air courtyard, terrace, or patio, you can take a cue from brilliant Mediterranean country homes and surround outdoor fountains, pools, rose gardens, or dining areas with tinted cement walkways inset with blue and white stones or blue and white geometric tiles from Morocco or Mexico. Rustic gray-blue unglazed quarry tiles or blue slate dimension stones are other striking ways to add blue to your home's outdoor living areas.

There is an endless variety of outdoor furniture available today, which enables you to interpret your personal style and colors in a contemporary, traditional, or country fashion. Contemporary furnishing styles include sleek steel-framed motel chairs in aqua or pale blue as well as synthetic wicker chairs in white or cobalt. Country and traditional homes can be graced with lovely garden benches, rockers, chairs, and tables made from teak, redwood, pressure-treated pine, or kiln-dried oak as well as with white or teal-blue cast-iron settees, chairs, and tables. Elegant cast- or wrought-aluminum designs can add international flavor to your outdoor rooms, mirroring the romantic furnishings of Arabian courtyards and Parisian cafés. You can also revive wooden furniture with fresh coats of Mediterranean blue, turquoise, or indigo paint.

Beyond the porch or within the courtyard walls, blue and white gardens are perfect places for heart-to-heart talks and leisurely breakfasts accompanied by birdsong. It's been said that a blue garden is good for the body and soul, since gazing at a sea of blue flowers can reduce your body temperature, slow your pulse rate, and quiet your appetite. By introducing white flowers into your garden, you add visual contrast, yet you maintain the graceful aura that only blue can radiate.

When designing a garden "room" in your favorite colors, you can literally take your love for blue and white to new heights. Tall trellises, pergolas, and arbors can simulate walls for morning glories, roses, and clematis to climb, while stone or tile pathways can suggest rustic floors under the sky's eternal blue ceiling. Garden furnishings provide a place to relax and enjoy the beauty of the outdoors, while sculpted ornaments of Buddhas, sprites, or mythological animals lend gracious personality. The most exciting aspect of designing a blue and white garden sanctuary is, of course, selecting an assortment of beautiful blue and white flowers to create your own tapestry of color, texture, and shape.

There's a wide variety of delicate and hardy blooms in this palette from which to choose, and it's wise to read a few gardening books and magazines to find out which flowers will thrive best in your climate. Classic blue posies for beds and borders include forget-me-nots, pansies, blue flax, lobelia, Veronica, and blue phlox. These stand out when they are surrounded by snowy lily of the valley, baby's breath, sweet William, and white violets. For cottage gardens, a mixture of exuberant white and violet irises, blue hydrangea, delphinium, larkspur, blue salvia, Canterbury bells, and the turquoise-hued Himalayan blue poppy can contrast elegantly with white roses, lupines, shasta daisies, and hollyhocks. As Henry David Thoreau said, "Heaven is under our feet, as well as over our heads." This was never more beautifully illustrated than in the enchanted blue and white garden.

Above: BLUE CORNFLOWERS AND PURE WHITE HYDRANGEAS COMPLEMENT THE SKY BLUE OF THIS SIMPLE PLANK TABLE AND ITS MATCHING BENCH. THE TERRA-COTTA VASE AND THE BRICK FLOOR PROVIDE A WARM CONTRAST TO THE COOL BLUES AND GREENS OF THIS GARDEN SPACE.

Opposite: PURE RED AND YELLOW ARE WARM HUES, WHILE BLUE IS REFRESHINGLY COOL. YET SOME BLUES SEEM WARMER BECAUSE THEY CONTAIN A TOUCH OF YELLOW, SUCH AS THE STRIKING BLUE-GREEN OF THIS SUNROOM'S ARMOIRE AND TILED FLOOR. **Above:** FROM THE PATTERNED TABLECLOTHS TO THE FINE CRYSTAL, CURVACIOUS WHITE CHAIRS, AND TINY LAMPSHADES, THIS ALFRESCO SETTING BLENDS SEAMLESSLY WITH NATURE, ECHOING THE GRACEFUL BLUES OF SEA AND SKY.

Opposite: This Mediterranean home's romantic courtyard is highlighted by a contemporary fountain fashioned from azure blue tiles. The terra-cotta pots of flowers add warmth to this magical setting. Azure was a popular wall color in Pompeii and Herculaneum, the ancient Italian cities whose treasures, excavated in the 1770s, inspired the vivid palettes and neoclassical designs found in Regency, Federal, and Empire decors. **Above, left:** In sun-drenched regions where homes are often painted a brilliant white or cool sherbet hue, it's common to color doorways in a deep, vibrant blue. In the Middle East and in some Native American communities, doorways have historically been painted blue to ward off evil spirits. **Above, right:** Because bright sunshine can overwhelm pastel hues, this Mediterranean-inspired loggia is done in earth tones, highlighted by a dazzling blue doorway and a simple, contemporary chair.

Left: A WASH OF APOTHECARY BLUE ENLIVENS THIS TALL COUNTRY FENCE, WHILE SPOTLIGHTING A DAZZLING GARDEN OF SNOWY WHITE FLOWERS. **Opposite:** THE DETAILS OF THIS HOME'S FAÇADE PAINT A PICTURE OF TRADITIONAL REFINEMENT. THE FANLIGHT OVER THE FRONT DOOR, THE VICTORIAN-STYLE IRON FENCE, AND THE BLUE AND WHITE COLOR SCHEME REFLECT AN APPRECIATION FOR CLASSIC ARCHITECTURAL DETAILS AND COLORS.

Opposite: BLUE-VIOLET AND SNOW-WHITE DELPHINIUM ARE THE STARS OF THIS LUSH, VERDANT GARDEN.

Above: IN THIS EXQUISITE GARDEN "ROOM," VISITORS FEEL A SENSE OF SERENITY, FOR LOOKING AT AN EXPANSE OF BLUE FLOWERS CAN SLOW THE PULSE RATE AS WELL AS DELIGHT THE SOUL. NOTE HOW THE WHITE FLOWERS AND THE PORCELAIN PLANTERS PROVIDE CONTRAST TO THE PALE AND DEEP BLUE BLOOMS.

Welcoming Rooms Serenaded in Blue

As the gateway to your home, your entryway is a place for daily comings and goings as well as emotional reunions and farewells. Down the hall, your living room or family room serves as a mecca for socializing and relaxing. Whatever your decorating style, a blue and white scheme can bring timeless beauty and color magic to each of these welcoming rooms.

Regency and Federal decors favor the bright French Empire style, so they share similar wall coverings, paint colors, furnishings, and window treatments. Regency and Federal entryways often feature flagstone, varnished wood, or mosaic floors and delicately proportioned neoclassical furnishings. Typical furnishings and accessories include shield-back chairs, gilded tables and mirrors, and chandeliers and torchères.

Regency and Federal drawing rooms can carry out a blue and white theme through resplendent white fireplaces covered with delftware tiles or neoclassical carvings; gracious solid or striped damask upholstery on Grecian couches; blue Aubusson carpets; and layered window treatments that include muslin undercurtains, Wedgwood blue or deep blue silk curtains, and Gothic scalloped valances with tassels. Traditional wallpapers include imitation marble, blue and white Regency stripes, sprigged florals, and blue and gray scenic wallpapers from China or France. Favored paint colors include Federal apothecary blue or cream and such Regency medium blues as sapphire, cerulean, or cobalt. Porcelain vases and urns by Wedgwood, Minton, or Spode reinforce the tranquil color scheme.

High-style Victorian entry halls and parlors often employ dark and light palettes of blue and white. An entryway done in a traditional deep blue embossed wallpaper is the ideal background for gilded mirrors and framed prints, an ornate mahogany table graced with a Tiffany lamp, a blue velvet chair, and an Oriental carpet in

Opposite: IN THIS INVITING REGENCY-STYLE LIVING ROOM, BLUE AND CREAM TOILE DE JOUY WALLPAPER AND FABRIC HARMONIZE WITH NEUTRAL CARPETING AND COMPLEMENTARY PILLOWS. GENTLE LIGHTING AND DEEP PINK FLOWERS ADD WARMTH.

sapphire and gold. In the living room, the ceiling might be painted white or pale blue, while the walls could be covered in a blue and white striped wallpaper, accented by light blue molding. Windows can have lace undercurtains topped by pale blue or rose chintz curtains and a blue fringed valance. Other blue touches could include an Oriental carpet, gilded Rococo Revival chairs, a settee upholstered in a pale blue damask, and a mahogany whatnot filled with Chinese porcelain and delftware.

Country-style entryways are less formal than those in traditional homes, yet they exude a gracious ambience. Country entry hall floors can be done in terra-cotta or dimension stone tiles, natural wood, or wood that's been painted or stenciled. Walls may be whitewashed or painted in pastel or medium blues. Decorative wall accents include stenciling, wallpaper borders, blue or white wainscoting, and a painted dado rail. Simple furnishings are best, such as old wooden benches, cast-iron chairs with blue and white gingham cushions, and antique coatracks.

A bright mood can be created in American country living rooms and family rooms with cream-colored walls highlighted by blue trim, stenciling, or wallpaper borders. Wooden floors may be topped with blue braided or hooked rugs, and windows graced with simple white shutters. Key color accents include a Prussian blue camelback sofa topped by an indigo and white quilt, Windsor chairs with calico cushions, and cobalt-glazed crocks filled with wildflowers.

The hallmark pastel blue walls of many Scandinavian country living rooms invite precious light to radiate throughout the home. These walls are often embellished with tongue-and-groove cladding or painted floral borders. Bleached wooden floors are accented with striped runners, while windows wear wispy muslin or lace swags. Traditional Scandinavian country furnishings are a joyful mix of contemporary blonde or painted wood pieces and treasured heirlooms. Common patterns for sofas and pillows include blue and white stripes and ever-popular ginghams. Key accessories include delftware, brass or wrought-iron candlesticks with thin white candles, and pots of summery red geraniums.

In French country homes, strong colors and earthy textures are everywhere. Thick stone or clay living room walls are often left radiantly white, but they can be tinted lavender or sky blue. Ceilings often reveal exposed beams, and floors radiate warmth through dark wood planks or terra-cotta tiles topped with cobalt blue floral rugs. Windows are barely dressed in lacy café curtains, swags, or wooden shutters. Comfort is offered by an assortment of curvaceous walnut or fruitwood furnishings and cozy upholstered chairs. A traditional wooden armoire, hand-painted or carved with botanical motifs, is typically the focal point of the room. Another key French country furnishing is the rush-seated banquette, a bench that can be topped with pillows in azure blue and white checks, paisleys, and traditional Provençal cottons.

In Mediterranean country living rooms, thick stone walls and ceilings are whitewashed, while trim is painted a brilliant blue to provide contrast. Brick, flagstone, or tile flooring is appropriate, as are sisal mats and brightly hued rugs. Sofas and chairs are often made of heavy, ebony-hued wood and sit close to the floor, where the air is refreshingly cool. Other common furnishings include rustic chests and tall cupboards for storage. Colorful accessories include cobalt blue and white pots filled with plants and flowers, turquoise and white wall hangings, and sky blue and white striped or checked pillows.

Like country settings, contemporary decors celebrate simplicity and vibrant hues. A minimalist blue and white entry hall might feature white brick walls and a pale azure ceiling with blonde parquet or white marble flooring. Contemporary furnishings include gleaming metal chairs, torchère-style lamps, and a glass-topped table displaying a clear or blue glass bowl filled with irises. In the living room, an ultramarine ceiling might be softened by white walls, or one gallerylike royal blue wall could be surrounded by vanilla walls and ceiling. Modular furniture in solid cobalt or cream can be grounded by a textured sisal rug. Other important touches include primary-color paintings, sleek marble tables, white lamps, blue glass candlesticks, white vertical blinds, and accent pillows in red, green, apricot, and yellow.

Above: A SHRINE TO NATURE'S BEAUTY, THIS AMERICAN COUNTRY LIVING ROOM'S WINDOWS RISE UP TO CAPTURE THE SUNLIGHT, WHILE THE EXPOSED BEAMS REFLECT THE RICH PATINA OF WEATHERED WOOD AND THE FIREPLACE OFFERS THE TEXTURE OF OLD STONES. BEAUTIFUL BLUE AND WHITE FURNITURE AND CHINESE PORCELAIN RECALL THE MANY HUES OF THE SKY, WHILE THE TALL ARMOIRE AND RED ORIENTAL CARPET RADIATE WARMTH.

Left: THE SCANDINAVIAN LOVE OF SIMPLE YET FUNCTIONAL FURNISHINGS IS REFLECTED IN THIS BACK-DOOR HALLWAY, WHERE THE BLEACHED WOODEN FLOOR HAS BEEN STAINED WITH AN ULTRA-MARINE ANILINE DYE AND SEALED WITH MARINE VARNISH.

Right: Glowing with the golden sunlight of late afternoon, this front room's powder blue and ivory color scheme seems positively warm. The delicate shell stencil on the chair takes its inspiration from the nearby ocean.

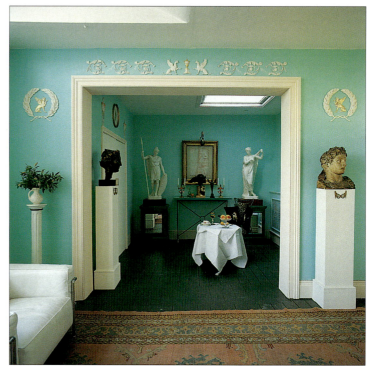

Above, left: THE CURVACEOUS FRUITWOOD CHAIRS AND TABLE, INTOXICATING FRESH FLOWERS, CHINESE PORCELAINS, AND INDIGO WALLS SUGGEST A FRENCH COUNTRY MOOD IN THIS DELIGHTFUL FOYER. **Above, right:** GRACEFUL STATUARY AND NEOCLASSICAL MOTIFS ADORN THIS FORMAL PALE TURQUOISE AND WHITE LIVING ROOM. **Opposite:** THIS FAMILY ROOM IS ENERGIZED BY SAND AND SURF HUES AND AN ECLECTIC DECOR THAT BLENDS CONTEMPORARY FABRICS, MEDITERRANEAN FLOOR TILES, THE SUNFLOWERS SO BELOVED IN FRANCE, AND ART INSPIRED BY NATIVE AMERICAN CULTURES.

Opposite: IN THIS ELEGANT MEXICAN HOME, BLUE AND WHITE FURNISHINGS AND DETAILS PROVIDE A REGAL AMBIENCE APPROPRIATE FOR THE DISPLAY OF TREASURED FAMILY HEIRLOOMS. **Right:** FOR CENTURIES, BLUE AND WHITE HAVE ADDED BEAUTY TO FABRICS, FURNITURE, WALLPAPERS, FLOOR TREATMENTS, AND MYRIAD ACCESSORIES. HERE, AN ECLECTIC AMERICAN LIVING ROOM CELEBRATES THE PATRIOTIC FIRE OF RED, WHITE, AND BLUE AGAINST A BACKGROUND OF VIBRANT SAPPHIRE. **Below:** THE BLACK AND WHITE FIREPLACE OF THIS TRADITIONAL LIVING ROOM PRESENTS AN APPEALING CONTRAST OF DARK AND LIGHT COLORS. SO, TOO, DO THE VIVID CHECKS OF THE COZY CHAIR AND CURTAINS, FOR BLUE AND WHITE MAKE AN UNDENIABLY STRONG COLOR COMBINATION.

Above: Inspired by the lovely blue and white porcelain that China is famous for, the pictorial fabric used for the chaise, throw pillows, and curtain trim brings vitality and charm to this pristine white living room.

Opposite: Anchored by a solid cobalt blue sofa and sky blue walls, this American country living room mixes stripes, checks, and florals in a spirited blue, white, and yellow decor.

Blue Sky Kitchens and Dining Rooms

As the heart of the home, the kitchen is often a multipurpose room for preparing and eating meals, socializing, watching television, and engaging in hobbies. And, despite our busy lifestyles, the dining room is still a treasured place in our homes, for it reminds us to take time to enjoy the pleasures of entertaining friends and family.

Kitchens can be enlivened by using blue and white on almost every surface. A wide variety of scrubbable wallpapers and semigloss paints are ideal for this highly trafficked room. Some popular flooring choices include vinyl sheet or tiles; ceramic, stone, and terra-cotta tiles; and richly speckled terrazzo made of marble, colored glass, and stone. Blue and white can also capture attention when used in the sink backsplash, countertops, appliances, textiles, and small accessories.

The walls and floor are ideal places to include color in the dining room. Solid blue or blue and white patterned wallpaper can add subtle or flamboyant flair, providing a textured background for paintings, lighting fixtures, and sideboard displays of colorful china and glassware. As

the "fifth wall" of your dining room, the floor can be covered with a luxurious azure Oriental or Aubusson carpet, a blue braided rug, or a neutral sisal rug.

Regency- or Federal-inspired kitchens are often painted apothecary blue or cream, or are papered with such patterns as eagles, laurel wreaths, or the Napoleon bee, while the walls in the dining room generally have the same treatment as those in the living room. Federal kitchens might have a blue-hued pine hutch and a gate-leg table with Windsor chairs, while Regency-style kitchens can be graced with a collection of porcelain in a gilded cupboard and floral prints hung with ribbons. In the dining room, both design styles commonly showcase a marble fireplace with Greek motifs and a mantel displaying Chinese ginger jars. Sumptuous furnishings include a neoclassical satinwood table and chairs, a matching sideboard and china cabinet, and such accessories as torchères, a gilded mirror, and ancestral paintings.

Victorians preferred an entirely white kitchen, but modern interpretations of the style often include one other

Opposite: Blue, white, and yellow make up a surefire color scheme for an energetic kitchen. This breakfast nook gleefully mixes contemporary lighting with American country chairs and flooring, primitive carved birds, and a variety of new and old dinnerware.

color. Classic Victorian kitchens have white, mahogany, or oak cupboards with glass fronts and porcelain knobs, as well as oak pedestal tables and chairs, lace curtains, blue and white ceramic or parquet floor tiles, and hanging lamps with colored or frosted glass globes. Kitchen walls can have pale blue or cream semigloss paint or a blue floral wallpaper above white wainscoting, while a dining room looks splendid in a deep blue Rococo, chintz, or Arts and Crafts wallpaper. The typical dining table is mahogany clothed with lace or linen and set with fine silver, crystal, blue and white china, and perhaps a vase filled with cabbage roses. The matching chairs and the windows might wear royal blue velvet, and the floor can be graced with a sapphire-hued Oriental carpet.

American and Scandinavian country kitchens and dining rooms share a love of painted wooden furniture, muted colors, ginghams, sprigged floral fabrics, and simple window treatments. American kitchen walls may be whitewashed or covered with a country floral or checked wallpaper, while the floor might be wood, terra-cotta tiles, or dimension stone. Blue highlights can include a display of antique tins and glassware, a braided rug, and cornflower blue countertops on blonde wood cabinets. In the Scandinavian kitchen, walls and furnishings are often painted pale blue, while the focal point of the room might be an armoire with rosemaling. A simple wooden table and chairs would be dressed in a gingham tablecloth and cushions, and the bleached wooden floor could be stenciled with blue and white checks and topped with a throw rug in one of the primary colors.

Both the American and Scandinavian country dining rooms might be outfitted with antique wooden tables and chairs; china cabinets full of blue and white porcelain, delftware, graniteware, or glassware; simple wrought-iron candlesticks; pale blue or cream painted walls; and lace panels on the windows. Suitable American country accessories include a blue and white patchwork quilt used as a tablecloth, stoneware crocks filled with wildflowers, and needlework samplers or folk art. Classic Scandinavian touches include an antique blue and white tiled stove, a curvaceous gilded standing clock, and a Swedish Rococo sideboard.

The sunny Mediterranean region is a magical place for alfresco dining and rustic, romantic decorating. The kitchen and dining areas are often combined in one open living space. White plaster walls are decorated with arches, native tiles, and azure woodwork and shutters. Furnishings include iron or black wooden tables, cabinets, and rush-seat chairs. Terra-cotta floors are topped with striped woven rugs, and accents such as turquoise and white ceramic pots filled with vibrant flowers and wooden bowls brimming with local produce grace the large, airy rooms.

In French country homes, kitchens commonly feature terra-cotta floors, whitewashed plaster walls with beamed ceilings, or walls done in petite floral or striped wallpapers. Work surfaces are often set with blue and white tiles, and the wooden tables and chairs wear viva-cious Provençal fabrics. Unique kitchen accoutrements include a panetière (vintage bread box), hanging copper pans, wire baskets, and enamelware pitchers. Nearby dining rooms enchant with their long wooden tables, rush-seat chairs with carved floral designs, and elegant armoires and china cabinets. Their terra-cotta floors contrast nicely with blue floral rugs, and chandeliers and candles illuminate the cream or white walls.

The contemporary kitchen or dining room offers both style and convenience. You can choose from an endless array of colorful cabinets, countertops, and appliances in such hues as royal blue, cobalt, gray-blue, and teal. There are also myriad ceramic tiles, lighting fixtures, flooring, window and wall treatments, and textiles to choose from. Contemporary kitchens and dining areas can be ultramodern or an updated version of a traditional or regional style. With a blue sky palette to pull it all together, you can even mix and match elements from a variety of styles.

Right, top: THIS AMERICAN COUNTRY KITCHEN IS A CHARMING VISION IN WHITE. THE RUNNER AND CHAIR CUSHION ADD RICH BLUE ACCENTS, WHILE THE CABINETS, CANE-SEATED STOOL, WICKER CHAIR, AND WOODEN FLOOR ADD TEXTURE. THE OWNERS' LOVE OF BARNYARD ANIMALS IS CELEBRATED IN THE DISPLAY OF COLLECTIBLES ABOVE THE KITCHEN WINDOW.

Right, bottom: THIS WINE CONNOISSEUR'S KITCHEN SPEAKS FRENCH COUNTRY THROUGH ITS DECORATIVE TILES, AS WELL AS ITS SPARKLING WHITE CUPBOARDS, CHARMING BLUE GLASSES, AND BOUQUET OF FRESH FLOWERS.

Above, left: BY ITSELF, WHITE CAN SEEM COOL OR CLINICAL, BUT WHEN COMBINED WITH BLUE, IT CREATES A SENSE OF JOY, PURITY, AND SOPHISTICATION, AS IN THIS VIBRANT MEDITERRANEAN COUNTRY DINING ROOM AND KITCHEN. **Above, right:** THIS CONTEMPORARY KITCHEN ECHOES THE COUNTRY PENCHANT FOR BLUE AND WHITE CHECKS THROUGH ITS PLEASING TILED COUNTER, WALLS, AND ACCESSORIES. **Opposite:** COBALT BLUE COUNTERTOPS, YELLOW AND CORNFLOWER BLUE TILES, WARM WOOD, AND COLORFUL ACCESSORIES CREATE AN OUTGOING MOOD IN THIS CONTEMPORARY KITCHEN.

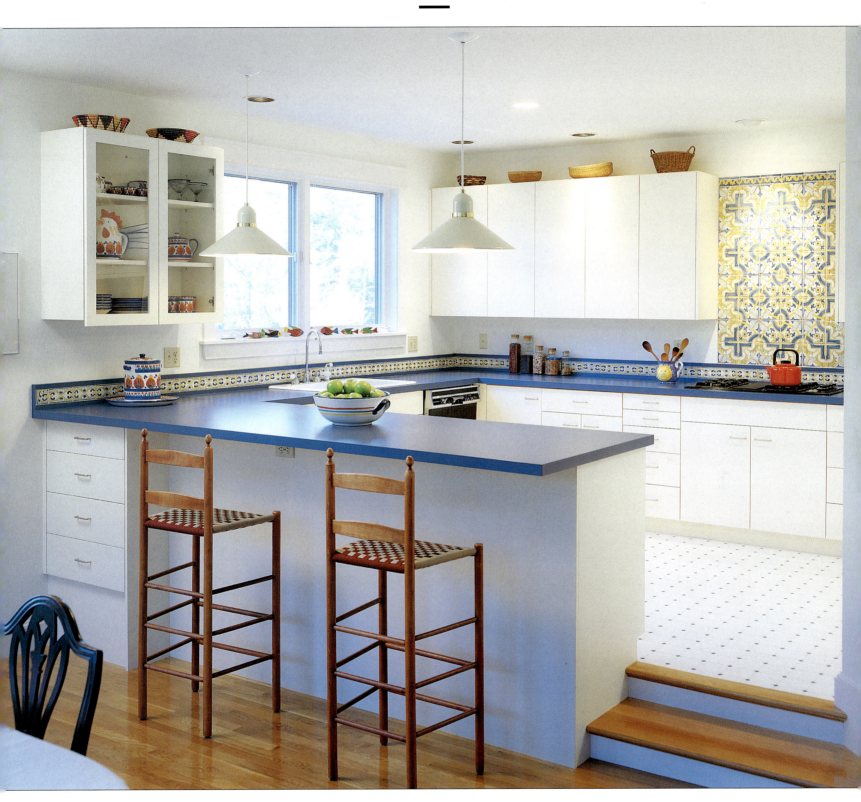

Opposite: DAZZLING "MAJOLICA BLUE" AND RED TILES ADORN THIS KITCHEN'S FLOOR AND WALLS. BEAMED STUCCO WALLS AND SIMPLE LIGHTING FIXTURES AND ACCESSORIES PROVIDE COUNTER-POINT TO THE ROOM'S FESTIVE PATTERNS AND HUES.

Right: VIBRANTLY COLORED SPANISH TILES SURROUNDING A VINTAGE BREAD OVEN ARE THE FOCAL POINT OF THIS MEXICAN COUNTRY KITCHEN. THE WHITE STUCCO WALLS, DEEP BLUE CABINETS, AND DECORATIVE CANISTERS ENHANCE THE ROOM'S CELESTIAL THEME.

Opposite: THE SHIMMERING MIDNIGHT BLUE FLOOR ENHANCES THE SERENE AMBIENCE OF THIS BREEZY MEDITERRANEAN COUNTRY DINING ROOM.

Above, left: ENTERTAINER DANNY KAYE ONCE SAID, "LIFE IS A GREAT BIG CANVAS." SO, TOO, ARE EACH OF THE ROOMS OF OUR HOMES, INCLUDING OUR OUTDOOR LIVING SPACES. THIS MEDITERRANEAN COURTYARD IS AN EXQUISITE ALFRESCO "PAINTING" THAT DELIGHTS THE EYE WITH RICH BLUE GLASSWARE, SPARKLING WHITE PLATES AND LINENS, LUXURIANT PINK BLOOMS, AND FRESH FRUITS IN A RAINBOW OF COLORS. **Above, right:** THE NEOCLASSICAL SHELL IS A POPULAR ARCHITECTURAL MOTIF IN MEDITERRANEAN-STYLE HOMES. THIS LUMINOUS BLUE WALL SHOWCASES A BUILT-IN DINING ROOM CUPBOARD WHERE A TREASURED COLLECTION OF CHINA IS DISPLAYED.

Above, left: COLLECTIONS SHOULD BE DISPLAYED AND ENJOYED, AS THIS KITCHEN HEARTILY ATTESTS. IN TRUE AMERICAN COUNTRY SPIRIT, WOODEN CABINETS AND EARTH-TONED TILES PROVIDE A WONDERFUL BACKDROP FOR DAZZLING BLUE AND WHITE DISHES AND GRANITEWARE, AS WELL AS A RUSTIC BASKET AND CHERISHED ROOSTER.

Above, right: THE CORNER OF THIS ROMANTIC FEDERAL DINING ROOM SPEAKS OF RELAXED ELEGANCE, THANKS TO CHECKERED CHAIR CUSHIONS, A BASKET OF FRESH FLOWERS, A MIX OF BLUE CHINA, AND A VINTAGE BLUE AND WHITE QUILT. **Opposite:** TIME STANDS STILL IN THIS FEDERAL-ERA DINING ROOM, WHICH IS GRACED WITH A LOVELY BAY WINDOW AND FIREPLACE. A VARIETY OF BLUES IS OFTEN FOUND IN SUCH A TRADITIONAL SETTING, FROM ETHEREAL SKY BLUE TO RICH ROYAL BLUE, AND EVEN THE GREEN-TINGED APOTHECARY BLUE, A PROMINENT HUE FOUND IN GEORGE WASHINGTON'S HOME AT MOUNT VERNON.

Ocean-Inspired Bedrooms and Bathrooms

It's de rigueur to decorate a bedroom and bath in the same serene maritime color scheme, perhaps even spotlighting boats, lighthouses, whales, or seashells in your decorating theme through wallpapers, fabrics, and accessories. Whatever design motif inspires you, blue and white should be used to color large areas of the bedroom and bath, such as walls, floors, window treatments, bed dressings, and bathroom fixtures.

Traditional bedrooms are outfitted with elaborate blue and white decors, while country and contemporary bedrooms are often decorated simply and sparingly. The bed and its accoutrements are usually the focal point of the decor in any bedroom. Federal and Regency bedrooms may feature a curvaceous neoclassical Empire sleigh bed, a four-poster bed with graceful turnings and a straight canopy, or a low "field" bed with an arched canopy. Traditional bed hangings often use up to sixty yards (55m) of such fabrics as indigo and white toile de Jouy or sapphire and cream chintz or silk, as well as summery cotton stripes or prints. In the Regency bedroom, white voile might be draped from a gilded corona above the bed. Delicate tables, chairs, chaise longues, and chests of drawers also furnish the room. The blue and white theme repeats in the striped or floral wallpaper, toile upholstery, and Aubusson carpets.

During the Victorian era, if a bedroom faced north, it was often decorated in a deep blue striped, floral, or foliage wallpaper, while a sunnier exposure called for pastel wallpapers in blues and whites. A typical Victorian bedroom can include a brass, iron, or wooden spool bed

Opposite: A GARDEN OF SENSUAL DELIGHTS, THIS BEDROOM INSPIRES A MOOD OF TRANQUILITY WITH ITS CASUAL MIX OF FORMAL AND WICKER FURNITURE, ITS COMFORTING BLUE AND WHITE QUILT, SOFT CARPETING, FRESH FLOWERS, AND THE MESMERIZING SIGHT, SOUND, AND FRAGRANCE OF THE OCEAN.

draped with a lace coverlet or a crazy quilt, a wooden floor covered with area rugs, an upholstered chair or settee, a night table with a stained glass or fringed period lamp, lace curtains, and several framed paintings or prints and knickknacks.

The American country bedroom provides blissful comfort with warm wood, woven wicker, or sturdy brass or wrought-iron furniture. Medium or deep blue and white accents can include heirloom patchwork quilts as well as hooked, braided, or rag rugs. Windows often wear

Above, left: POWDER BLUE WALLS ENHANCE THE ALLURE OF THIS REGENCY-STYLE BEDROOM'S MURAL OF ANCIENT RUINS. THE ANTIQUE DRESSER AND FRAMED ARTWORK ADD TO THE ROOM'S HISTORIC AMBIENCE. **Above, right:** THIS TEENAGER'S RETREAT ENCHANTS WITH ITS AMERICAN COUNTRY MIX OF FABRICS, FLOWERS, WARM WOOD, NAUTICAL PAINTINGS, OLD LICENSE PLATES, AND A BELOVED CHILDHOOD FRIEND.

demure lace or sprigged floral curtains, which echo print wallpapers or stenciled borders. Country accessories include baskets full of blue wildflowers or blue glass bottles filled with daisies and forget-me-nots.

The Scandinavian country bedroom offers an even simpler interpretation of the soft celestial palette. The room charms with a cozy built-in bed or a freestanding wooden bed with a blue gingham, calico, or striped bedspread and matching bed and window curtains, ice blue walls with blue wooden shelves, bleached wooden floors with striped runners, and, for cheery contrast, a red or yellow painted chair.

A typical Mediterranean bedroom is a cool, white sanctuary. The room usually features whitewashed walls and wooden floorboards covered with sheepskin or woven rugs. Windows have muslin curtains or azure blue shutters. Furnishings may include a simple iron bed topped with a white crocheted comforter, a wooden cupboard for clothing, and a rush-seat chair. Accessories are kept simple, such as a decorative ceramic hand basin on the wall for a splash of color and a treasured painting or religious icon.

The French country bedroom is usually furnished with an elaborately carved armoire, a *lit bateau* (wooden boat bed) or a painted iron bed, and a wooden or wrought-iron chair and table. Windows might be veiled with net or lace curtains and a polished floor made cozy with a woven rug. In true Provençal tradition, walls are covered with layers of wallpaper and borders. Key wallpaper choices include fresh yellow and cobalt blue or dusty blue and white patterns such as miniature florals, trelliswork, dots, twigs and leaves, and ribbons. The wallpaper could be complemented by similar blue-hued patterns in the bed linens or accent pillows.

The contemporary bedroom has license to employ everything from the deepest to the most demure shades of blue and white, keeping in mind the golden design rule that "less is more." Midnight blue walls can make a large room seem cozy, while off-white walls with a pale azure ceiling will open up a small space. A restful ambience can be achieved with blue carpeting, wooden or metal furnishings, glass- or marble-topped tables, vertical blinds or Roman shades, recessed lighting, simple torchères, textured pillows, and a contemporary painting or two.

Today's half- or full bath can easily echo the decor of any bedroom by matching or using similar fabrics, wallpaper patterns, furnishings, and accessories. A variety of contemporary and reproduction products exist to outfit the bathroom, as many homeowners today want to transform their baths from strictly utilitarian spaces for bathing and grooming to luxurious retreats designed in a favorite period or regional style. Every color of the rainbow is available in today's selection of fixtures, flooring, wallpapers, ceramic tiles, and durable semigloss paints.

Opposite: THE SLATE BLUE WALLS AND WHITE BEDS AND LINENS OF THIS RETREAT PROVIDE COUNTERPOINT TO THE PROFUSION OF BOTANICAL DESIGNS IN THE FRAMED PRINTS, BEDSPREADS, AND UPHOLSTERED FURNITURE. **Above, left:** TAKING COLOR CUES FROM ITS RADIANT TILED FIREPLACE, THIS BEDROOM'S BLUE AND WHITE THEME IS IDEAL FOR ITS SUNNY SOUTHERN EXPOSURE. THE MEDIUM BLUES OF THE BEDSPREAD, WINDOW TREATMENTS, AND ARMCHAIR ADD A SENSE OF COOLNESS, AS DO THE WHITE DRESSERS, PALE BLUE WALLS, AND WHITE CEILING. **Above, right:** IT'S IMPORTANT TO REMEMBER THAT WHEN DECORATING WITH BLUE AND WHITE, THE SATURATION OR BRILLIANCE OF BOTH COLORS SHOULD MATCH TO CREATE A SENSE OF HARMONY. THE DUSTY BLUE OF THIS AMERICAN COUNTRY BEDROOM'S CURTAINS AND BEDSKIRTS BLENDS PERFECTLY WITH THE GRAY-BLUE RUG AND SERENE WHITE WALLS.

Left: THIS FORMAL BEDROOM, FILLED WITH RICH FEDERAL-ERA FURNISHINGS, IS BATHED IN NATURAL LIGHT AND FRESH ISLAND BREEZES. THE HANDSOME SHUTTERED DOORS AND THE QUILT ON THE BED ADD A REGAL BLUE AMBIENCE TO THIS SHADED SANCTUARY.

Left: OFTEN, TODAY'S AMERICAN COUNTRY ROOMS OFFER AN ECLECTIC BLEND OF FURNISHINGS AND ACCESSORIES. THIS BEDROOM SUCCESSFULLY MIXES DARK- AND LIGHT-TONED PERIOD FURNISHINGS WITH CONTEMPORARY CORN-FLOWER BLUE WALLS AND A CREAM-COLORED CEILING. THE ROOM'S BLACK-FRAMED BOTANICAL PRINTS STRIKE A MODERN CHORD, WHILE THE WOODEN FLOOR, PATCHWORK QUILT, AND BRAIDED RUG CELEBRATE TRADITION.

Opposite: A SEA OF BLUE FLORAL CARPET AND WEDGWOOD BLUE AND WHITE FABRIC COLOR THIS TRADITIONAL BEDROOM. THE FEDERAL-ERA FURNISHINGS INCLUDE A FULL-TESTER BED, A GRACIOUS HIGH CHEST, AND AN ELEGANT SETTEE.

Left: THE SUN AND STARS PRESIDE OVER THIS FAIRYTALE-LIKE BEDROOM RETREAT. THE GRACE OF THE CLOUDS ON THE CEILING IS REFLECTED IN THE WISPY BLUE WINDOW DRAPERY. AN ANTIQUE ANGEL, SEVERAL RABBITS, A MINIATURE CHAIR, AND A VENERABLE METAL BED ADD TO THE MAGIC.

Below: MEDITERRANEAN COUNTRY HOMES ARE COMMONLY PAINTED WHITE, WHILE THEIR WINDOW FRAMES AND DOORS ARE RESPLENDENT IN SUCH VIBRANT SHADES OF BLUE AS TURQUOISE, COBALT, OR AZURE. HERE, A VIVID BEDROOM DOORWAY OPENS ONTO A SUNLIT TERRACE.

Above: THIS LOVELY MIRROR DOESN'T NEED A FRESH COAT OF PAINT. ITS CHARM LIES IN ITS AGED PATINA, WHICH ATTESTS TO YEARS OF FAITHFUL SERVICE IN THE PURSUIT OF BEAUTY. THE BEDROOM'S PASTEL BLUE WALLS, OLD-FASHIONED DRESSER WITH GLASS PULLS, SEA GREEN TIN WIND-UP ALARM CLOCK, AND VASE OF BLUE HYDRANGEAS ALSO REFLECT SIMPLER TIMES.

Below: GLOSSY CERAMIC TILES IN WEDGWOOD BLUE AND INDIGO CREATE A DRAMATIC COUNTERPOINT TO THE WHITE AND BLONDE OF THE CEILING, FLOOR, AND TUB SURROUND. THE COLOR PALETTE OF THIS BATHROOM MAKES SUCH A STRONG STATEMENT THAT FEW ACCESSORIES ARE NEEDED.

Above: THIS SPACIOUS BATHROOM RETREAT PAMPERS WITH ITS CONTEMPORARY BATHTUB IN STRATOSPHERE BLUE TILES, EXPANSIVE CABINETS, PLUSH CARPETING, AND SUPERB VIEW OF THE GREAT OUTDOORS.

Opposite: IN THIS ELEGANT BATHROOM, THE CABINET, OVAL MIRROR, GINGER JARS, AND TILED FLOOR SUGGEST A VICTORIAN MOOD, WHILE THE STRIPED VALANCES AND FORMAL SIDE CHAIR LEND REGENCY FLAIR. COBALT BLUE GLASS TUMBLERS AND JARS ADD A CONTEMPORARY TOUCH.

True-Blue Accessories

"A thing of beauty is a joy forever." When we think of the inner and outer beauty of our homes, John Keats' poetic words ring true. Even the little things add splendor, for treasured blue and white accessories paint our rooms with personality and, in many cases, a sense of history.

Whether we exhibit ginger jars on rustic dressers or display favorite plates and platters on the walls, blue and white china is a stellar accessory that's perfect for any decor. Between the 1500s and 1800s, spices, fabrics, and radiant blue and white porcelain were exported from Cathay (known today as China) to Europe and America, where only the wealthy could afford them. Around 1735, the process for making china was duplicated by potters in Meissen, Germany, and by 1750 the English were creating such enduring blue and white china patterns as Blue Willow, Canton, Fitzhugh, and Nanking. During the Victorian era, a great deal of blue and white china produced in Staffordshire, England, was exported to America, where it became a symbol of status. Another desirable accessory is antique flow blue china, produced primarily in England from the 1830s through 1910. Flow blue features a cobalt, navy, or steel blue underglaze that is slightly blurred from the firing process.

Luminous blue glass pitchers, vases, and candlesticks can also add immense charm to windowsills and table-tops in your home. One of many styles of collectible glassware is Depression glass, manufactured by numerous American companies between 1920 and 1940. Of the more than twenty-five colors made, common Depression glass hues include pink, green, and amber. Some less frequently manufactured colors are turquoise, peacock blue, ultramarine, cobalt, and ice blue—all sought after today for their beauty and rarity.

Hand-painted tiles are another vibrant way to introduce sea and sky colors to your favorite indoor and outdoor spaces. Tiles that are porous are sensitive to extreme cold and are unable to withstand water penetration, so you might use them around your fireplace and hearth.

Opposite: WHEN DISPLAYING BLUE AND WHITE ACCESSORIES, YOU CAN ADD VISUAL PUNCH BY INTRODUCING VIBRANT YELLOW, ORANGE, OR RED ACCENTS, SUCH AS THE FLOWERS ON THIS KITCHEN DRESSER. BLUE AND WHITE IS A SOCIABLE DUET THAT BECOMES EVEN MORE APPEALING WHEN HIGHLIGHTED WITH WARM COLORS.

Tiles that are nonabsorbent are hard and able to withstand moisture and drastic temperature changes, so they make ideal sink backsplashes and garden pathways. Enchanting tiles to look for include blue and white delftware from Holland, turquoise or cobalt and white tiles from the Middle East, and blue majolica tiles from Italy, Portugal, Spain, and Mexico.

A symbol of thrift and creativity, the handmade American quilt is also partial to a blue and white palette. In the early 1800s, almost every American quiltmaker made at least one indigo and white quilt. The color combination was considered harmonious, and indigo dye's superior ability to withstand repeated washings had been renowned since the Colonial era, when indigo was the most widely used coloring agent for homespun fabrics. Several quilt patterns that are traditionally done in blue and white include Irish Chain, Feathered Star, Hole in a Barn Door, and Drunkard's Path.

Around the world, several stunning fabrics that were created centuries ago continue to inspire a variety of traditional and country-style blue and white pillows, curtains, tablecloths, wallpapers, and dinnerware. These include French toiles de Jouy, which feature single-color pastoral, Oriental, or historic scenes on a light ground; English glazed cotton chintzes bedecked with blossoms, ribbons, ivy, birds, and butterflies; and French Provençal cottons with tiny floral, geometric, or paisley patterns and sunny Mediterranean hues.

Today's toiles de Jouy were inspired by the copperplate fabrics designed by Christophe-Philippe Oberkampf, a Bavarian artisan who manufactured his decorative cotton-linen fabrics in Jouy-en-Josas, France, in the late eighteenth century. Chintz is frequently associated with English country decor, but it actually originated in India, where artisans lovingly created hand-painted or hand-blocked cotton and linen fabrics. These flora and fauna fabrics have been exported to Europe since the seventeenth century. Like chintz, the captivating fabrics that we associate with Provence today take their inspiration and motifs from the handmade prints that originated in India centuries ago. For more than two hundred years, vivid Provençal "Indienne" fabrics have been woven and printed in Tarascon, France, to emulate the unforgettable beauty of the landscape of southern France.

Another classic accessory that is often found in French and American country decors is graniteware, also known as enamelware or agate ware. Examples of graniteware include such utilitarian items as water pitchers, coffeepots, and canisters that were made of cast iron or sheet metal and coated with enamel. Alluring blue and white designs included swirls, checks, stripes, speckles, floral motifs, windmills, and sailboats. From the late 1800s through 1940, graniteware was produced throughout Europe and America. Blue and white graniteware is very popular among collectors today, for in the antique business blue apparently attracts more buyers than other colors.

Legendary artist Pablo Picasso once said, "Why do two colors put next to one another sing?" When you lavish your home with blue and white furnishings and accessories, you can see and feel the perfect harmony to which Picasso referred. The boldest or softest blues and whites enchant us, reflecting our enduring love of the sea, the sky, and the precious blooms of our gardens.

Below, left: WHETHER YOU DISPLAY OLD BLUE GLASS BOTTLES, CONTEMPORARY VASES, OR SEVERAL DEPRESSION GLASS PITCHERS ON YOUR WINDOWSILL, WHEN THE SUN BREAKS THROUGH YOUR COLLECTION WILL SPARKLE LIKE SAPPHIRES. **Below, right:** DRUNKARD'S PATH IS A BELOVED CLASSIC QUILT PATTERN FOR GOOD REASON. SIMPLE BLOCKS—EACH IS A SQUARE CUT DIAGONALLY IN HALF BY A SEMICIRCLE—IN JUST TWO COLORS CREATE A STRIKING AND SEEMINGLY COMPLEX DESIGN. THIS BEAUTIFUL EXAMPLE CERTAINLY DESERVES ITS PLACE OF HONOR ON THE WALL.

Above, left: THIS CLOSE-UP OF A SCANDINAVIAN COUNTRY LIVING ROOM WALL DEPICTS A PAINTING WITHIN A PAINTING. THE LOVELY SEASIDE SKETCH IS ENCIRCLED BY A HAND-STENCILED WALL, A TIME-HONORED ALTERNATIVE TO WALLPAPER. **Above, right:** REMINISCENT OF NINETEENTH-CENTURY FLOW BLUE CHINA, THIS DELICATE DINNERWARE OFFERS WINSOME FLORAL DESIGNS THAT ARE COMPLEMENTED BY THE BUTTERFLY TABLECLOTH AND SPRINGTIME GRAPE HYACINTHS.

Opposite: LIKE A SUMPTUOUS STILL-LIFE PAINTING, THIS ALFRESCO TABLE SETTING MESMERIZES WITH ITS COBALT GLASS DINNERWARE, SILVER AND CRYSTAL ACCESSORIES, COMPLEMENTARY BLUE FABRICS, AND LUSH GARDEN PLANTS.

Opposite: A casual blend of several blue and white fabrics and wall coverings can look splendid in any decor when the intensity of the blues match. Here, several medium blue plaid, gingham, and toile de Jouy accessories sing in harmony. **Below:** In many Scandinavian country kitchens, bleached wooden floors are stained or painted with a blue and white checkerboard motif for added color and design.

Above: A close look at this country bedroom's checked drapes reveals their reversible floral theme, as well as an idyllic pastoral view from the window.

Above, left: AN ANTIQUE BLUE AND WHITE TILED STOVE TAKES CENTER STAGE IN THE DRAWING ROOM OF THIS SWEDISH PAVILION. THE ELEGANT CHAIR BESIDE THE STOVE DATES FROM THE RULE OF GUSTAV III OF SWEDEN IN THE EIGHTEENTH CENTURY, WHEN FURNISHINGS HAD SOFT, FLUID LINES AND THEIR PAINTED SURFACES REFLECTED NATURAL LIGHT. SUCH FURNISHINGS EMULATED THE DECORATIVE FRENCH ROCOCO STYLE. **Above, right:** THE VERSATILITY OF PAINT AND THE VITALITY OF BLUE AND WHITE SHINE THROUGH IN THIS HOME'S HAND-PAINTED FAUX TILE FLOOR BORDER, DESIGNED TO ECHO THE WALL'S REAL TILES AND THE DECORATIVE TABLE. **Left:** AS BUILDING BLOCKS OF THE FRENCH COUNTRY KITCHEN, THESE DECORATIVE TILES DELIVER PRACTICAL AND PRETTY ARCHITECTURAL VERVE WITH A CLASSIC FLORAL MOTIF.

Right: BLUE AND WHITE PORCELAIN IS PERENNIALLY POPULAR BECAUSE IT COMES IN SEVERAL VIBRANT SHADES OF BLUE, BLENDS WELL WITH BOTH WARM AND COOL COLORS, AND IS UNMISTAKABLY CLASSY.

Sources

SOURCE DIRECTORY

Furnishings

The Bombay Company
Call for the nearest
dealership.
(800) 829-7789

Broyhill Furniture Industries
Call for the nearest
dealership.
(800) 3-BROYHILL

Carolina Patio Warehouse
58 Largo Drive
Stamford, CT 06907
(800) 672-8466

Charles P. Rogers Brass
& Iron Beds
55 West 17th Street
New York, NY 10011
(800) 272-7726

Crate & Barrel
Call for the nearest
dealership.
(800) 323-5461

Dalton Pavilions
20 Commerce Drive
Telford, PA 18969
(215) 721-1492

Drexel Heritage Furnishings
Call for the nearest
dealership.
(800) 916-1986

Ethan Allen
Call for the nearest
dealership.
(800) 228-9229

French Country Living
10205 Colvin Run Road
Great Falls, VA 22066
(800) 485-1302

Kohler Co.
Call for the nearest
dealership.
(800) 456-4537

SOURCES

Pier 1 Imports
Call for the nearest
dealership.
(800) 447-4371

Plain & Fancy Custom
Cabinetry
Call for the nearest
dealership.
(800) 447-9006

Spiegel
Call for the nearest
dealership.
(800) 345-4500

Thomasville
401 East Main Street
Thomasville, NC 27361
(800) 650-1669

Wellborn Cabinet, Inc.
38669 Highway 77
Ashland, AL 36251
(800) 762-4475

Accessories
The Antique Quilt Source
385 Spring View Road
Carlisle, PA 17013
(717) 245-2054

Chuctanunda Antique Co.
#1 Fourth Avenue
Amsterdam, NY 12010
(518) 843-3983

Marimekko
698 Madison Avenue
New York, NY
(212) 838-3842

The Masters' Collection
40 Scitico Road
Sommersville, CT 06072
(800) 222-6827

Period Lighting Fixtures
167 River Road
Clarksburg, MA 01247
(800) 828-6990

Pottery Barn
Call for the nearest
dealership.
(800) 922-5507

Sur La Table
1765 Sixth Avenue South
Seattle, WA 98134
(800) 243-0852

PHOTOGRAPHY CREDITS

©Phillip H. Ennis: pp. 24 (Designer: Country Floors), 68 bottom left (Designer: Patricia Falkenburg)

The Garden Picture Library: ©Janet Sorrell: p. 15; ©Ron Sutherland: pp. 22, 23

©Michael Garland: p. 46 left (Designer: Peggy Butcher)

©Tria Giovan: pp. 33 right, 35, 64 right, 67 right

The Interior Archive: ©Tim Beddow: pp. 9 left, 40 left, 57 right; ©Simon Brown: pp. 33 left, 66 (Designer: R. Banks-Pye); ©Tim Clinch: p. 50 left; ©James Mortimer: pp. 30 right (Designer: Mary Goodwyn), 65 (Designer: Nina Campbell); ©Simon Upton: p. 60

©image/dennis krukowski: p. 30 left

©David Livingston: pp. 10, 31 (Designer: Sharon Campbell), 50 right, 52 (Design by: The Wiseman Group), 58 left (Designer: Nancy Scheinholtz)

©Maura McEvoy: p. 57 left

©Eric Roth: pp. 6 (Designer: Benn Theodore Inc.), 34 (Designer: Nancy Alexanderson), 39 top (Designer: Kalman Construction), 47 (Designer: Maggie Duncan), 53 left

(Designer: Kalman Construction), 55 (Designer: Benn Theodore Inc.), 68 top right

A.G. Speranza: ©Marina Papa: p. 19 left and right

©Tim Street-Porter: pp. 2 (Designer: Brian Murphy), 17, 18, 28 (Designer: Brian Murphy), 32, 42 (Adamson House, Malibu), 43, 44 (Designer: Brian Murphy), 45 right, 58 right

©Steve Terrill: p. 21

©Brian Vanden Brink: pp. 12 (Architect: Tony DiGregorio); 29 (Tom Catalano Architects), 36, 41 (Architects: Scholz & Barclay), 59 (Mary Drysdale Interior Design), 63 right (Robert Currie Interior Design)

©Dominique Vorillon: pp. 54 top, 54 bottom (Designer: Kimberly Latham), 56 (Designer: Janyce McCarthy)

©Jessie Walker Associates: pp. 27 (Designer: Colette McKerr), 39 bottom (Designer: Donna Aylesworth, Akins & Aylesworth Interiors), 46 right (Designer: Mary Ellen C. VanBuskirk), 67 left (Designer: Janice Russillo)

©Elizabeth Whiting & Associates: pp. 9 right, 16, 20, 40 right, 45 left, 48 (Designer: Alexandra Stoddard), 53 right, 63 left (Designer: Joan Peters), 64 left, 68 top left, 69

INDEX